An Old-Fashioned 1 2 3 Book

VIKING

ELIZABETH ALLEN ASHTON

An Old-Fashioned 1 2 3 Book

ILLUSTRATIONS BY

JESSIE WILLCOX SMITH

V   I   K   I   N   G

VIKING
Published by the Penguin Group
Viking Penguin, a division of Penguin Books USA Inc.,
375 Hudson Street, New York, New York 10014, U.S.A.
Penguin Books Ltd, 27 Wrights Lane, London W8 5TZ, England
Penguin Books Australia Ltd, Ringwood, Victoria, Australia
Penguin Books Canada Ltd, 2801 John Street, Markham, Ontario, Canada L3R 1B4
Penguin Books (N.Z.) Ltd, 182–190 Wairau Road, Auckland 10, New Zealand

Penguin Books Ltd, Registered Offices: Harmondsworth, Middlesex, England

First published in 1991 by Viking Penguin, a division of Penguin Books USA Inc.

1   3   5   7   9   10   8   6   4   2

Library of Congress Cataloging in Publication Data
Ashton, Elizabeth Allen.
An old-fashioned 1-2-3 book / by Elizabeth Allen Ashton :
illustrated by Jessie Willcox Smith.   p.   cm.
Summary: A counting book featuring the art of
Jessie Willcox Smith, a popular and acclaimed illustrator
in the early part of the twentieth century.
I S B N 0 - 6 7 0 - 8 3 4 9 9 - 8
1. Counting—Juvenile literature. [1. Counting.]
I. Smith, Jessie Willcox, 1863–1935, ill.   II. Title.
III. Title: Old-fashioned one-two-three book.
QA113.A84   1991   513.5′5—dc20   [E]   90-42789   CIP   AC

Printed in Hong Kong   Set in Goudy Old Style

An Old-Fashioned 1 2 3 Book

Come along and follow me

Through all the verses, then

In each picture you will see

Each number, one through ten.

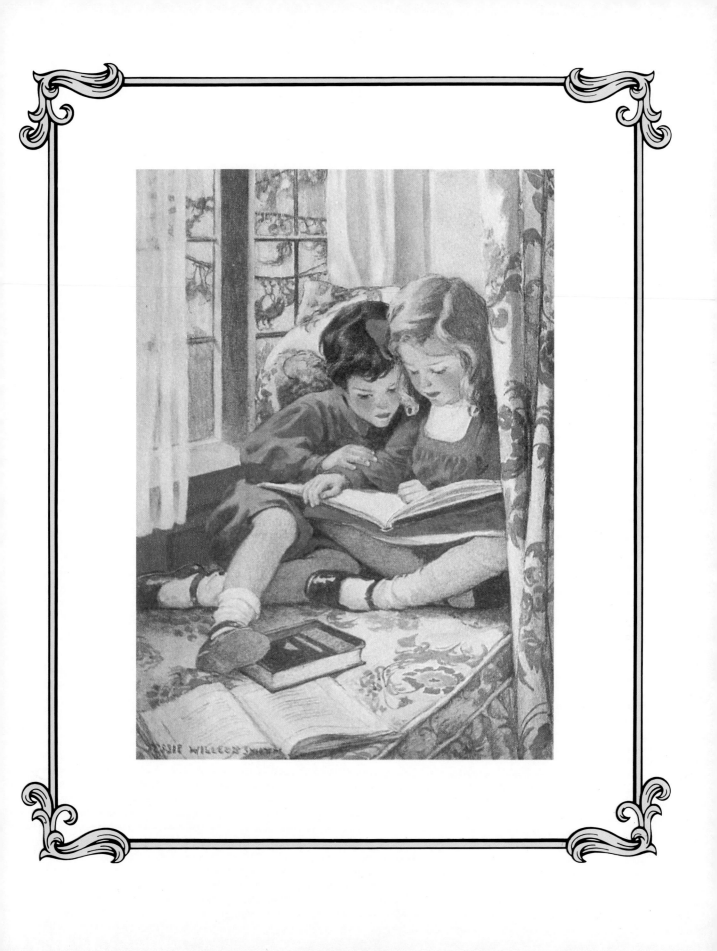

Floating on a salty wave,

Jenny rides with Paul.

Reaching out, Paul tries to save

His one red rubber ball.

2

Terry and Tess are just the same,

Though two, they look like one.

Identical twins enjoy their game

For two can have more fun.

3

Three bears met beneath a tree:

Father, Mother, and Teddy.

Jenny counts them, 1, 2, 3,

All here? Her picnic's ready!

Heather and Jill, Jill and Heather

Kneel upon the grass.

Two new friends make four together

In a lake's looking glass.

5

I've five bright tulips in a row.

I tend them every day,

They nod their heads and say, "Hello!"

As soft winds make them sway.

There is a special place I know,

A secret hideaway,

Where fairies dance as breezes blow.

Can you find six at play?

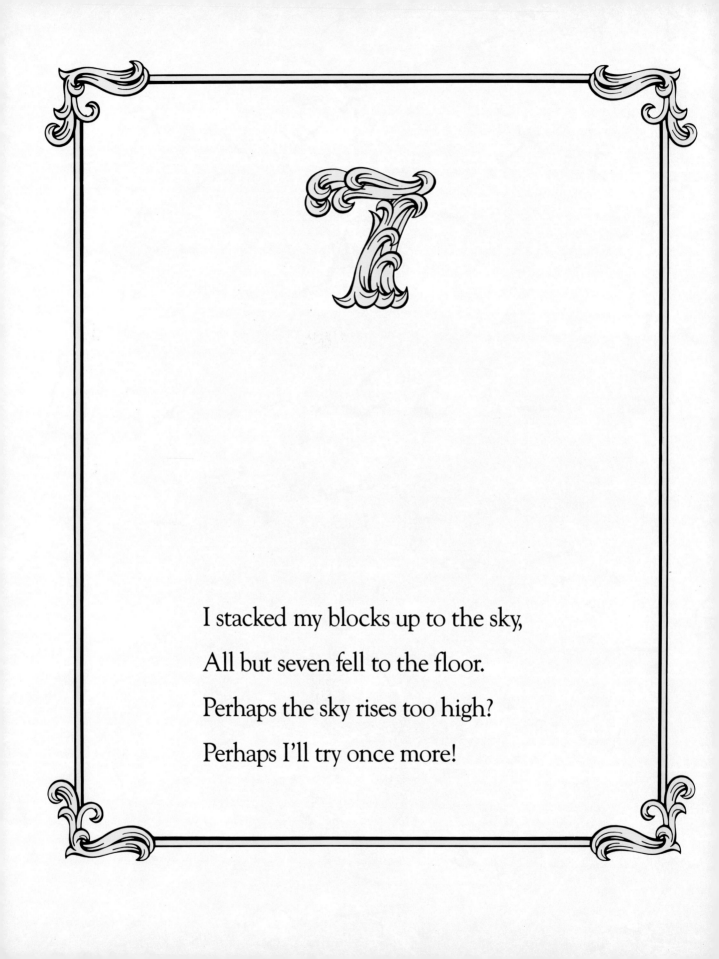

7

I stacked my blocks up to the sky,

All but seven fell to the floor.

Perhaps the sky rises too high?

Perhaps I'll try once more!

Like flowers in the air they soar,

Floating before her eyes.

Sally claps her hands in joy

For eight bright butterflies.

Teacher gathers the children near,

A fairy tale she'll tell,

Nine happy children laugh and cheer,

Then it's time to listen well.

10

As I work, who's watching me?

My ten dolls in a row.

They all attend quite patiently

As I teach them to sew.

Now number ten is not the end, so

Let's count away the hours,

And number all the flowers that grow

And each petal on each flower.

Or count the stars that twinkle bright,

Up in the evening sky.

And soon we'll say a soft good night,

With a number lullaby.